POEMS

Artwork

POEMS
Dorothea Millett
ARTWORK
Edward Millett

Regent Press
Berkeley, California

Copyright © 2026 by Edward Millett

ISBN 13: 978-1-58790-731-9
ISBN 10 1-58790-731-3

First Edition

Manufactured in the United States
REGENT PRESS
www.regentpress.net

Remembering

I met Dorthea at Lowell high school in San Francisco back when it was on Hayes St at Masonic. And then I met her again at a Halloween party at the San Francisco Art Institute. She was already a good poet at 19. Dorthea did not read her poems in public very often. She won a prize for the poem "Mediterranean" at College of the Holy Names. Dorthea had a bachelor's degree from the San Francisco State College in geology. She also had a master's degree in Anthropology.

Dorthea often writes about personal events from her life. Her ability to connect these with the impersonal and perennial is one of her strongest assets.

In the poem "The Ambassadors" there is a death event, a migration, as the entire poem involves a cultural change brought about by a shamanic transformation with man, animal, and plant.

In the poem "Prayer" she speaks about creative confidence, but also about the humility necessary to gain entrance to the archetypal and the always.

In the line "pieces of self" from the poem "The Ambassadors," we are reminded that we are constantly changing, reintegrating our wholenss. Our self is influenced by associations, our friends, everything including the food we eat. Resolution by eating, again from "The Ambassadors," somehow nourishes us the reader.

The line "Follow the night in the sun's receding" from the same poem lets us know that the night has not taken over here "in the sun's receding" but has become included in the day. The inner light, her inner light, is what is being followed. Follow the night to get back to the light.

The line "His hand at the industrious grain" reminds me of the reference to farming in John Keats poems. The poem about William Blake is also one of my favorites. I intentionally put it at the back.

— *Edward Millett*
October, 2025

An Introduction by Way of a Series of Notes
by Peter Sherburn-Zimmer

From notes from my journal: reading this poet, is she a prophet or a technician? Am I looking at what she reveals or how she presents her vision? I can't always separate the two, nor should I feel I need to. Poem by poem I look for technique and look for vision in these four packets of poems.

Start with the packet of poems beginning with THE PARABLE OF RELIGIOUS PARALELLISM. The images, so traditional throughout, even unto the peeling skin of the serpent. The theme, ecumenism, is very rational, intentional and explicit, in contrast to the mystic 'topical: illumination, fire, ecstasy...so hard to reconcile, here captured in the crystalline imagery. I end with the sense that this is a poem about religion rather than a more direct expression of the mysticism it draws upon...a difficult gulf to cross for any writer. I begin and end thinking instead of feeling: my intuitive understanding is not challenged here, note: Excuse me, if I am addressing her rather than her editor in my comments. It seems the more appropriate approach for this work.

SRI RAMAKRISHNA The mix of acceptance and rejection throughout engages the reader in the mix of her or his feelings, surely, the human puts the angels in their place, as we find in Rilke's Duino Elegies as well. The earthiness of the pigs and the seed-pods is never abandoned here...even with the open characterization of the body as a 'cage'.

"The bright companion" [In these, there is so much the woman speaking, even if for me, the man cannot hear.] — this makes my commentary presumptuous. "A CARNIVAL OF DISINTEGRATION" her description of birds flying stuck for me. And her insight into Blake and evil was worth meditating seriously on. Dorothea's poem FOR NED— the first in the packet in which she brought feeling from the reader, 'reaching for the shape: I wonder why Ned would have some foolish literary critic, like me, with his irrelevant 'standards' and arcane strategies of reading, try to write about these poems he loves. The atmosphere of the poems is more like fantasy literature so far than like mythology for me, that is, more like Tolkien than Homer. The more I read, the more I am pleased to have read.

Then look at a packet of poems beginning with AT THE DOOR.
PRAYER I associate this with Hermes Trismagistes, ['thrice sung poetl'] — probably what Richards would call an irrelevant association. Looking for the object of her prayer. Then I would have been proud to write:

The measure of poetry begins
With a real bird in the real world
Beginning to sing.

On the mysterious white mountain
The snow glides into water
And in two days
We at the foot also hear it.

In this poem, 'begins' such a telling word...she gives us a version of reality as the beginning of the poetic process, not as its result. In THE HOLY HERMIT RE-ENTERS THE WORLD I the oracular oratory that is often the diction of amateurish poetry. I also went through a phase of announcing what I was saying when I spent that forty years of writing what I call bad poetry before I became a poet. That is, before I learned to read my own poetry as if it were written by someone else. 'The Mountain Spring flowers' Here, by placing the two observations beside each other, the poem shows its meaningfulness more strongly than it would if she had spelled out their relation., Trying to name them explicitly would have hidden the vision. Simplicity is here richness. Hurt [stone]: spring flowers. If we look at "Love Within, Love in the Greeting," we find a woman poem, something woman that a man may witness in human compassion at most. She presents her earthiness: deeper and more lucid, although I don't care for the title, since it doesn't get me into the poem.
AND THIS ALSO Some of her poems, although quite good, are be-

yond my commenting, since they are in a genre different from what I might know about. The poem that sounds like a narrative play, for instance, like Eliot's play poems or Stevens' play poems...pieces I would not comment on because I don't understand the dynamics they use. I guess I should just say I like the thing and leave it at that instead of responding like a critic.

There is a fair measure of surprising turns of thought in her work. We find hints of synesthesia: as in 'This world is in visual song.' from "Her hair was ripe". This is a very unusual trait in any writing. She writes, sometimes, directly about mystical understanding, 'beyond experience,' as in VOTIVE POEM.

If we move to the packet of poems beginning with untitled poem beginning, "The winged lion, manheaded, lies," the lines I find most poignant among these poems.

> 'Build a tent of sorrow
> To Keep out the rain of stars.
> Painted jars and drums...
> All that is...Contains
> Some evil, sealed in a circle.'

Such wisdom here, constrained within her meditation on the body of the sphinx calls forth, through some subterranean association, the terrifying dustiness of 'The Land of the Living' from the Sumerian's Epic of Gilgamesh. However, again, this might be my mind associating with irrelevant texts. Coming back to Dorothea's POEM 'Beyond our lives, and dim.' — we find she does know how to close a poem with a line that justifies our reading through the text. With SHIVA we come to the word for much of Dorothea's poetry. That may or may not attract the reader. Not every reader of poetry seeks fable. However, this particular poem is as delicate as the trembling butterfly wing-world it describes. And with INTO THE SECRET, she tells us, 'We come as strangers to ourselves. I THAT is so easy to forget or ignore.
Looking at the packet of poems beginning with ENLIGHTENMENT,

Dorothea expands the range of what we can expect to hear from her.

Simple, common and joyous: ENLIGHTENMENT. She presents us with her vision of a dervish leaf-like, bird-like park detritus, swept away. Later, we hear 'through the voices / Of our astonished yearning. I In these lines from a poem she revised at least five times we can hear why she didn't give up on it.

I came this far to get to the point at which Dorothea's work demanded I reach into myself to accept her vision. To my mind, the best poem of the bunch I read is her mad response to her own madness entitled THE SENSUALIST IS A LIE. I But one must choose his own poison. Certainly, so many of her poems are so written by a woman from a woman's perspective it might be seen as an insult to have a man, any man, myself included, interpret them, let alone evaluate them (as we always do when we read). Still, here we find the passion she covers over in those poems anaesthetized by the vocabulary of fable. Here we dwell among the monsters that the 'sleep of reason' dresses for daylight.

In GERMINATION again her acquaintance with despair overflows as it accompanies the taste of blood in her mouth...not a taste we like to remember, but one we cannot forget.

The Christmas scene of AS I COME HOME FROM THE STORE gives up both the 'mutated mythology' and 'Teenage tribal females' on the way to 'the carved oak door' ... overcoming the mere sentimentality that the reader might bring to the scene of the old fellow at the end of her little narrative. With JAZZ BABY Dorothea certainly puts in my mind photos of my mom as a flapper in the twenties. The life of fragments like [IN] PREHISTORIC TIME gives us the straightforward plea, 'If only I did not dream.' The problem of every poet!

Even in YGGDRASIL: WORLD TREE she touches on the necessities of mystic experience while restraining herself with the vocabulary of fable...knights, gardens, perfumed women...when her fear and her having 'put aside my mind' reach so much further than the traditional imagery. My reading of her pieces began and ended with her meditation on Blake, who 'most gently / spoke of evil.' And it is that she lived in a world in which she acknowledged evil but was still able to speak truth as she understood it that is her subtle accomplishment.

Finally, I find it interesting and intriguing that the pieces I prefer are those at the bottom of the pile and that the pieces that were most highly recommended to me turned out to simply not address my sensibilities. Such is the diversity of tastes, I guess. Other readers will find, I think, her diversity at times matched by her depth.

CONTENTS

REMEMBERING *by Edward Millett* v
AN INTRODUCTION BY WAY OF A SERIES OF NOTES
   by Peter Sherburn-Zimmer vi

POEMS *by Dorothea Millett*
A Dance on Bare Rocks 5
In Praise 6
All In the Sluice and Flow 7
Perhaps It Is The New Soul Rising 9
The Ambassadors 10
When Blake Saw 13
Poetry as Speech 13
The Acquaintance 14
The Sensualist Is a Lie 15
The Winged Lion, Man-Headed 17
Amid the Waist-High Poppies 18
Fire Walker 19
Man Bathing 20
Poem 20
The Marriage 21
Enlightenment 21
The Bright Companion 23
There Was Once a Man 24
Shiva 25
The Parable of the Religious Parallelism 26
Spectator 29
M.C. 30
Black Magic 31
The Amusement Park 33
The Medallion of Miraculous Happening 34
In Ancient Science 35
The Measures of Poetry Begins 37
For the Tomorrow Star 37
Room with Window 38
The Holy Hermit Re-enters the World 40
He Has Fallen 41
Te Deum 43

Dinner Party	45
And This Also	45
Beloved, the High Altar	46
Her Hair Was Ripe	46
Votive Poem	47
Kiev (1986)	47
Egil, Blind and Old	49
At Midnight, a Myriad of Small Sounds	50
Over and over, my hand	53
Love Within, love in the Greeting	`51
Lament For You	55
A Just Thing	57
Husbandry	59
Yggdrasil / World Tree	61
The Mountain Spring Flowers	62
Prayer	62
Old Confrontation	63
Irish Songs	65
To my husband Ned for the New Year 1968	65
Old Songs	66
Going Out, the Wind was Rising	67
For Ned	69
Who Will Break the Cherry Branch	70
They Flee From Me	70
The Convergence	71
Mediterranean	73
We Were	74
Masquerade By Day	75
Gather Together	77
To the Moan	79
As I Come Home From the Store	80
Dark Sabbath	81
Germination	81
At The Door	83
Poetry as Speech	83
Sri Ramakrishna	84
And Then	85
Jazz Baby	87
In Prehistoric Time	89
Mater Doloroso	90

Vacant Lot 91
Poem at the Cusp of the Year 91
Winter in San Francisco 93
Each Coat a Color, Each Room a View 94
A Dervish in the Park 95
Into the Secret 97 97
Crow Woman 99

ARTWORK by Edward Millett
Seven Spheres (2011) 4
Tai Chi Symbol With Full Moon 8
William Blake's Compass (1974) 12
Alchemical Man 16
Emanation [civer] 22
Tai Chi Symbol (1959) 28
A Yarn of Maya 32
Tai Chi Symbol 36
Going Down 42
Om Mani Padme Hum (1969) 44
Exuberance (1984) 48
Mandala With Snakes (1977) 52
Green Gyre (2023) 54
Circular Energy (2025) 56
Eye Flower Green Violet (2007) 58
The Crack Between The Two Worlds (1979) 60
Green Planet 64
Eye Flower Red, Blue 68
Turning Turning (2025) 72
Tai Chi Symbol (2025) 76
Paper Chase With Motorcycle (2019) 78
Paper Chase #1 (2019) 82
The Turning Wheel (2025) 86
Search (1978) 88
The Sailor Poet 92
Spiral Planet (2010) 96

SEVEN SPHERES (2011)

A Dance on Bare Rocks

My sea soul consecrates itself,
Whether I wish it to or not
Whether in good or unseasonable weather.
I carry the story of growth on my instep
Like the sharpness of a broken shell.
Beneath me, close, the black water
Flows in crevices
Splashes and slops . . .
Flickers of life surface there,
And I am curious, compelled by darkness to crouch down,
But my hand comes up only with seaweed.
Nevertheless, they have the mute friendliness of the dead.
I have no pity for them.
These gray rocks with white
Seagull droppings, slippery algae
Treacherous sliddings and crab snappings . . .
The sea never invites me, in fact
It is inhospitable.
But I come anyway.

In Praise

A big brown bear of relentless
Following, its
Great paws padding muddy earth, a
Thunderous flesh,
Immutable, ponderous, often humorous,
Absolutely ruthless.
Slowly takes into account
Every flash of rainbow
Belling fish,
A stone throw of birds toward winter,
not Exactly counting but
Noticing.
An old furry-burry,
A sleepy watcher of everything out from under its hair.
Running through the thin birch at beginning winter
With a snuffle toward the pine.
The old bear of self who thinks
Only when absolutely necessary
And then with a huge, brown creaking of his jaws

All In the Sluice and Flow

All in the sluice and flow of her tide-feelings
he entered. The alien thunder
 echoing caverns. What life turning under,
 to turn again
sea litter scattering strangely in morning light.

Rings of coffee mugs and smoke
blue reflections on the mirror
this comradeship, never to be erased.
We share the children
rolling like blond, thoughtless, happy dogs
an infinity that brings the sea air in
laid across the floor like a Persian carpet.

The ruin of public life . . . The pigeons
swoop through the lath and plaster of a
crumbling ethos.
At the edge of the sky a darkness . . . approaching
 on the diamond-bead of this one single moment
draw the inward breath.

TAI CHI SYMBOL WITH FULL MOON

Perhaps It Is The New Soul Rising

Perhaps it is the new soul rising
That pulls the tethers of my thought
Like a vast painted balloon.
It creaks ponderously
While I try to housekeep
In its earthbound basket.
I can imagine it-
Snap, snap, snap,
And there I am rising
Above the town, the trees, the crowd
Their faces suspended in astonishment
Like people in an old photo.

The Ambassadors

Forest, fern, hill of the oak

I take to my keeping.

Here, in the grass imbedded country

above the plain

 I nourish a plum tree

bent to the ground with black fruit.

And under that dark tree

the beasts of my mythology

move together with a wounded breathing.

In the valley it is

the day of the crow

whose doing is bound to the sun,

the seasons of man,

and his hand at the industrious grain.

Under the tree the blue raven

is opening his feathers on the wind.

And now he lifts to strike the crow,

leaving its crumpled body

like a sign to the others.

And now they go,

they migrate

Across the valley

Hungry, billowing

pieces of self, a carnival of disintegration.

Hairy hides, scraping together,

come to the mountain's creaking

past the devastated valley

open like a split melon.

Rung by rung of the day's ribs

climbing, these creatures

to follow the night in the sun's receding.

Forest, fern, hill of the oak

red mountain creaking

I send them out

to do my eating.

WILLIAM BLAKE'S COMPASS (1974)

When Blake Saw Visions Through the Shattered Pane

When Blake saw visions through the shattered pane
Of a morality, kaleidoscopically turning the light
On his own inner beauty, and saw
A world of demons eating their own poisonous
False piety,
He did not despair of it. In praise
He lived his days, and most gently
Spoke of evil.
It was the Evil themselves
That became enraged at it.

Poetry as Speech

A tapestry broidered with flowers
Fruits of all seasons, and alighting birds
All the beasts of the plenteous earth
So, If the gift of beautiful speech were given me,
Would I tapestry my god's temple
For pure love, and in the boldness of joy.

For the good god alone
Speech without this wrangling tongue
Pierced and cloyed in opposition;
Utter only the shape of the skin of silence.

The Acquaintance

Talking to him
Was like looking hard in an old mirror.
It was a glimpse of something always known
But never noticed before...
A conversation played out years ago
Into which the eternal juggler had entered
And subtly displaced the speakers.

I caught in a corner of my mind's eye
A picture of him
The gnomic personage of change
Dancing in caverns of the past
Singing the thousand voices of the days
With a high taste for comedy;
And I felt anguished, and betrayed.
I cried to him "lust
is the constant river.
It runs deeper
Than your hand can go."

To go there is an act of devotion.
That shore on which I stood, sir,
In my hag's hair coat
Does not admit the téte à téte you wished for.
It is not that, but a thorn Under the skin of the mind That maddens us
to hear.
And mad we come,
To sleep in the sand.
But in that sleep of reason monsters cope
Stripping the finery of flesh to deck their backs.
And drunken on this shore you stand alone
To throw yourself upward to the sun Or
lie down on the icy sand to play
A game of hunger in the whoreing bone.

The Sensualist is a Lie

Ride the white wind tonight and
Break a match on the rough shore
 For your tinder heart.
Look to the see, aches gull your despair
High into the spray wind from the
Grizzle of your see-weed throat.
Peer, goatface, into the cloudy eye of tomorrow.
Tickle her.
Giggle her past phosphor fire, sailors' bones,
Sleeping wormy galleons of brave destinies.
Tipple with her until she gives it up
Spews it on the floor, the promised
Amulet on which is etched the map
And words to the keeper of the gate
Of the city.
Be the great imposter bluffing his way to heaven
On the rump of an old metaphysical concept.
But no—already I see you
Climbing into a bottle
Corking yourself in
Like a desperate prayer to your own
True and seaward bobbly destiny.

ALCHEMICAL MAN

The Winged Lion, Man-Headed

The winged lion, man-headed, lies,
In the dead grass
He dreams of fat antelope, slaughtered
oozing from slits in their buff hides.
He rises heavily
And goes, like a broken, unreal thing
Across the sand.
Behind him, the mark of claws
And the delicate line, left by the tip
Of heavy wings

This brooding calm after violence
Leaves the world so still
That dead dreams come thronging back
From the soul's Egypt.

Our sight finds little to grasp
In the dark world
Gods step lightly;
Their heads rise in illumined yellow eyes.

Build a tent of sorrow
To keep out the rain of stars.
Painted jars and drums ...
All that is ... Contains
Some evil, sealed in a circle.

The sphinx rests in sand,
Its face to the sun
Its limping paws become desire
The body beyond death.

Amid the Waist-High Poppies

Amid the waist-high poppies, deep in dream
I grew in subtle fantasies of light
Cleaving under the golden sun
While all the flowers gaped
Their bright and languid sexual shape.
They printed on each breast, like fabric
Hammered on the flesh.
They wound royal and black mysteries
Against my thigh, and pierced my head
With orange, and the silent scream of red.
Within that garden, I the towering queen
Treaded the scent
Of intimate selves, and remembered
How some disaster of ancient
And personal proportions
Had caused me to leave my birthright,
My heritage and my throne,
These flowers of perception
Like withered starvelings on the frozen ground.

Fire Walker

Out of the dust of human futility
There rises such a flurry, a furiously red flower or
Flame, a little bright pain
That dances over the heads of the half-mad.
And it is this, this starry
Little protuberance of existence that
Conquers us in our most fortunate and secure
Hours, and gives us insight. Inside
A lake of arrested complexity we are carried
On the brink of a sharp, perhaps sapphire knowledge
That it is endless, this
Rising and falling and cracking of the human heart.
Without any end at all, but the flame or
Illumination which moves among the many figures of death,
Desire, the little and great births of things Is exquisitely fascinating and
brings to us a kind of Sentimental terror.

Man Bathing

Steaming back, the
Mysterious him
Underwater, the toes
Curling under his buttocks.
His chest, pink tits, his
Thin legs
Fine hairs drawn around the flesh,
The purple-brown water snake
Floating in the soft hair
Of his thighs—
All the water-bright flesh
And the eyes
Brown and serious as walnuts
Turning toward me, toward the land—
Merman.

Poem

On the pitiful air-the sorrowful time
The trees must move.
In summer, the finest season
We are born again
With greenest angels in the grain.
We tread the meadow stench
And rest, dizzy and golden
Admiring ourselves.
But still on the wailing air
The trees move
Beyond our lives, and dim.

The Marriage

In deep impoverishment, as from a field of war
She came to him.
And it was not pretty to see. The love she
kindled.
She wished to make a place of his bones,
Arced high, and virgin white,
Hers, her dwelling place.
What a passionate evil was there,
Angry her fingers reaching through.
The gray amenities.

Enlightenment

Like a garbage can
Rolled by the wind
It rings with hollowed out laughter.

Emanation

The Bright Companion

The bright companion I called you,
And let the veins in your wrists be my highways
Love, a body like unto a cave
I wish to hide in you
Swallowed by the sluice of your blood.
Nothing else equals this experience
Fish float and gull wheeling
Kisses that fount over sand and into the water
Or fern trickle, a moving shadow of
You, moving to me, your hand
Slowly opening my leg to plant
Life there,
It is life. There is no other.
O the very little stones give forth green
The very skies would answer you
calling

To complete
Is the wish of the leaf
Fruit into seed, and seed into fruit
A litany murmured in cellular prayer.
The woman and the children
Interweaving; the shadows
Carry them out of time beyond the
Garden
Back, back to the bright companion.

There Was Once a Man

There was once a man
Who saw the world
As though it were underwater.
In the morning the sun
Came through his window
And he swam in the waving shadow
Of the single thin tree on the street.
He liked best the mornings
When the heat spread in the air
(Which he thought water)
In clouds of dusty stars
These days were not often,
But the man was a man
Of great faith and joy,
And he thanked his flowing mother
For both the warm and the cold.
Now the man
Was not in the least mad--
He knew that no one else
Shared his watery views
But he was tolerant,
And above all silent,
Because it is hard to hear voices underwater anyway.
And so he would pass
Slowly through the streets
Until he got to his office,
Where he was paid by the hour
to copy letters.
He didn't mind copying the letters,
But it seemed foolish,
Because they would all wash away.
Never the less, he remained
Silent and tolerant,
And he always finished a day's letters
With a swoosh of his pen
And a lovely rippled smile.

Shiva

He sits in the far garden
His golden robes trembling, silk thin as breath
He is, in his own way, dancing.
Mindful of the garment
To its subtle edge,
And when it moves, he moves his mind with it.
He is in fact, a dancer among jeweled silences,
He is at the core of movement,
Still.
At the end of three thousand years
He will arise
And the world will tremble
Like the wing of a
butterfly Caught in the
hand.

The Parable of Religious Parallelism

Ultima Thule, Nirvana, and the Christian Celestium

All paint the door to the gate

With Seraphim.

Like old wood, weathered,

The ancient colors flaking off like pieces of an unstuck poster.

A dark tunnel they've climbed through,

The saints, who come back from the edges of their minds to tell us.

A chilly dark,

The end illuminated,

Shining like a jewel in the distance.

Come closer.

Do you see it?

The land inside the jewel,

With its shimmering fountains,

Its bright soft colors;

Warm air, flaming with amber-gold, violet, and red;

Do you see the snake

Ringed round the gate?

Dreamers white lotus crowning black emerald pools?

High on a hill, far off,

Trembles a dwelling of considerable proportions:

Jade palace, Minaret, Our Father's House.

From the golden door, do you feel the cold winds blow?
Looking at the empty dark, are you afraid

In paradise, the ecstasy of stone, sapphire-star hearted
Becomes crystalline
In the saint's fire.
But the heart with stone in it
Becomes all stone, with no fire star.

Have you seen, in the fairy tales of the brothers Grimm,
Or in pictures of Christ at the edge,
The tiny, little world inside the jewel?
From the time of first birth pang to the cradle of the moldering grave
This incorruptible illumination haunts us.
Our egos preventing us from wandering forever
 through these halls of jade
Until the body peels like the empty skin of the serpent.

TAI CHI SYMBOL (1959)

Spectator

This thinly brilliant aristocracy
Of morning skyline
Splits me lonely
would have windows
A little less wide.
Where are my old walls?
They were fine things to beat upon.
To be a warrior within walls is better—
A thick and discolored soul
Beating down its own battlements.

The windows then were tall
And narrow; I could see
Processions through them.
One sleepy dog, and a woman
Carrying flowers in her apron,
Three children and a wagon full of stones.
They had a truth between them.

Now it is all so big
I see nothing but the wide black earth
And the sky
Falling everywhere around in the morning.

M.C.

The jester turns —
His brows are white with age
Or powder
Or with both
His eyes are wide
And dreaming to the sharp
Unwholesome music of disfigured hearts.

He starts to dance —
He dances, as he must
No carnival of follies can proceed
Unless the convolutions of this grinning ape
Murmur a serpent into every ear
That folly's all the truth
And truth is such
As serves to bind the rag-patch
To the dancing bone.

He amuses no one Only the twirl
In the long mirror fixes him
To a jesting point
Too cruelly sharp
He cannot dance there long
The jester fades-the carnival's begun.

Black Magic

Through the halloween hours
Of the dark times
We moved and spoke
And frightened each other with too faithful
Masquerade,
We dipped fingers witchy with hunger
Into each other's paper maché hearts
And our hands came up
Suddenly bewildered With red wetness.
We fed
Each other's growing dark
With the dark within us,
And you, taking an apple from my thigh
Were in a game, and nothing lost
The apple not a treasured fruit.
And I; darted and tongued
The sticky sweetness of your mouth,
A honeyed despair.
To be thus, and the times of ghosts
And dead things, having no time,
Was all the play. We lay naked,
Needing no clothing from the rage
      in each other
Our self rage.
And as we lay
Stripped to our madness, the grinning truth
Watched,
And the night
Slowly went away from the window.

YARN OF MAYA

The Amusement Park

1.

The lights kaleidoscope a face:
A grinning sexless hag, end overlaid
The tear-stained oily blanche
Of Peirrot.

Mingling their public breath
Among the seas of cellophane,
A convict carnival, scarlet robed,
Parody the twisted mirror-men.

They march their legions
Between the eons of a waiting kiss...
They catch the shrieks end roller-coaster down the air
They grovel in ghastly humor
Under the empty matchbooks and the paper cups,
And dissipate along the beams
Of thinning night.

11.

At dawn the deadened sun reveals
A ferris wheel—
God's myriad eye
Strung out along a spiders web
Of steel, and spun upright.
A terrible chill has frozen shut
The machinery of Armageddon,
Leaving good and evil
Like amber caught revelers at mardi gras
Masked in silken black sophistication,
Unsolved and dissonant.

The Medallion of Miraculous Happening

Of the floating world of promise
A speck drifts against my horizon
An irritant perceived on the edge of the real world.
Becoming larger, bright, bloody
Like a light shown in the eye
the after-image veined
And full of curious intimacy...
So this disc was webbed,
Life flecked, filled with the fluid of the germinal seed,
And even so, rising like a sun,
A half-turn lifted flashed light.
The translucent pink
From yellow to the rattle of gold
Until a fist of gold hangs
With a metallic glint,
Blinding some inner sight.

In Ancient Science, Beautiful and Clean

In ancient science, beautiful and clean,
Man lived at the center of singing spheres
That danced in a golden round, below Heaven.
This celestial seed-pod ... Something shouldering up
A dirty and insistent head
Round, lewd, inquisitive eyes
Peering with intelligence out of an ape's skull
This cosmos in a tea-cup
Has been mourned in its departure by voices
Come singing down the mountains,
Come wailing from deserts, come
Shattered and limping out of cities.
True priests of a lost god, they
Mourn his going, they take up the clay pieces
Tenderly, breathing against
Man, I would dream a merry-go-round
With the best of you, thinking
In 3/4 time and parading the gilded
Wooden steed, his carved mouth
Forever parted in an ache of galloping, but
Far off, behind or
Beneath
I hear a litany of passing.

TAI CHI SYMBOL

The Measure of Poetry Begins

The measure of poetry begins
With a real bird in the real world
Beginning to sing.
On the mysterious white mountain
The snow glides into water
And in two days
We at the foot also will hear it.

For the Tomorrow Star

For the tomorrow star
Cometh into the valley.
The light of the world Is extinguished
In your eyes.
Your dream is other-worldly as the dawn,
As present and fruitful as air
Before rain.
Therefore do I love you,
And in this make my peace with the world.

Room With Window

The garden remains.
The rain
Asked at the windows,
Asked at the doors,
But we were there for human warmth—
The laying of a hand across
A night pale chest
To find the water path a hand might take
Down to the last places of dreaming.

All through love-making
Sounds of rain curtained our imagination
Of the peaceless garden.
Blind as the mouths of children
We were together,
And not a single star to worry us.

Before dawn I awakened
And you were going dark,
Riding some wet high horse
Through trees, through cliffs of your beginnings
Drinking the rain from your hands:
One. Single.
So drawn away that my hand felt the chill
Growing along your side.
Beyond your unmoving sleep
I saw the trees,
Separate,
Through the precise glass.

And the rain, which asked everywhere
Was in our garden

And had taken the garden away
Into the steady gray light of forever,
To feel it blossoming in droplets.

For every man there is somewhere
A garden of rain
Strewn to a silent abundance
With its fine, passionless,
Unshared fruit.

The Holy Hermit Re-enters The World

Nail my despair to a higher wall
That it may also strike fire at sunrise.
These mummified and cavernous eyes,
And thin mouth
Are wounds that slit
Its thousand-time remembered head.
 Now bleed gall and white excited
Expanses of morning.
Beginning now to unsee, foresee
Cellular conviction,
Raggedy leather of bone
Brooding into the wall
Becoming a protuberance of the stone,
Where the stone meets the insistent, trafficking air.

He Has Fallen

He has fallen
Upon the fields of life,
For he has taken the beautiful Black-eyed tormentress
For his wife.

A woman, then, with hair
Black, coiling down her back,
Breath that freezes the air
And kills with brittle perfection.
The shrew of the soul,
She has usury to bind him.
He cannot get rid of her image
In the mirror, behind him.

Oh buy and buy again, lady,
With him who will bargain with you.
Beauty withers,
The fine air gathered in
Billows with a putrid smell.
In their day's passing
They hardly look at one another.
They are, man and wife, one person.
In sameness there is no reconciliation.

GOING DOWN

Te Deum

The warm waterfall
Of Eros
Where he purifies his flesh
And lets his spirit rest
Shared with the water lilies
And the lovely women
In the shadows
The flowers expand, their odor spreads.

Eros nostrils flared
Must draw in the scent
And the dreaming of fleshy
flower as it opens, blooming
to die and shrivel.

The trees are also in flower and
they are visited by birds with
iridescent plumage.
They are melodious in their
love-making
They are desperate in their
tiny bodies.
All the beings of Eros are warmed
in undulations of desire
They are dissolving
In the center is Eros, full, fleshy,
 lovely, ever alive.

OM MANI PADME HUM (1969)

Dinner Party

The umbels of flowers share some resonance
With the final gong.

In the midst of it he jumped and said
He understood it, but
Then he forgot what, so
We went on drinking
While he went back to puddle his dark drunk brain
For phosphorescent spiders.

That it was common didn't mean It was simple. . .
He got lost, I mean.
Everyone started looking past him.

And This Also

And this also
Goes through me
heart, liver , sleepy soul
a cat's eye in the rib
I am the cow's calving barnyard
Of provincial fertility
Mewing and barking to the certain trough
Of affection . . . Rest

Come around and maybe I will
open doors, wrap curtains around your eyes
Hold your sleep under my breast
Like an old hen.

Her Hair Was Ripe

Great golden hosannas
And she was in Wake mellow and bird song
Swollen like a pear.
Take other winds, edge them
Toward the golden country,
Up, and mountain ward...
This world is in visual song.
She, the feminine self, fertile beyond desire,
Calls, calls penetration,
A growth to be worked
Upon the silky water-cell world
Bound by the wide horizon of her thighs.

Beloved, The High Altar

Beloved, The High Altar
Richly caved and painted longships prow
Heavy with furs from dark laplands winter store
A white falcon, caged and hooded, spitting
His ill temper;
Sail next the wind, cut next the bone of thought.
Under the laden olive branch
Another mystery stirs in its sleep.

The throat nearly breaks with song
Beloved, the high altar
Brief spring breathes over the mountain meadow.

Votive Poem

The well
beyond experience
Extends into mind
Water laps at the rim.
Tide pools of generation form
At the volatile edge.

The well remains.

Kiev (1986)

The slender woman
Walked through the bright rain
The umbrella
Translucent pink
Delicate steps

The lovely, dangerous rain
The teardrops
From half a world away

Beauty, break into my heart
And let me give my tears, also.

EXUBERANCE (1984)

Egil, Blind and Old

Chased from the hearth by the housewife
A dog with only the growl left
Still boasting more of his poems
Than his deeds at arms
The old barbarian.

Something precious, cradled under leaves
Hidden for the seeker, who comes
Bareheaded, barehanded, full of song
A stranger out of any place
Who sings all gatherings up to fate,
And has no voice himself save the river, raveling,
Comes to take up his place
Next the ghosts in the ruins of the hall.

At Midnight, a Myriad of Small Sounds

At midnight, a myriad of small sounds
The ropes, the scrape of wood against wood,
the scrape of oily water on the wind

A minute whirr of gull wings
Sounding as though they were wet with dark,
Heavy and resistant.
The fish boats creak like ghosts, and against the overcast
their spindle towers sway.
Nothing else of them is clear--
Mammoth and strange fish lie
writhing on their decks,
Or only the glove and jacket
Of the fisherman.
Indistinct, the line between the water
and the vessel changes with the light
As the fog shreds and piles before the moon.
And everywhere is the sound of water
Going in small places, going
out from the pilings with a sucking sound.

Love Within, Love in the Greeting

My body has something earthward to it
Now that I am again child-bearing.
Desire runs over me, like waters
Into a sea of which this mind is the shore;
And 1 dream the dense dreams of earth
Heavy with unworked met
secret with Jade.

Something of the curved planet turning in vapor
Lies behind my thought
My stillness is more still
My peace more like the very quiet plants.

While 1 am played upon by light
While light has entered into a covenent
With the dark.
While the sapphire's star focuses;

The jades luster becomes deeper
And more lucid.

MANDALA WITH SNAKES (1977)

Over and Over, My Hand

Over and over, my hand crosses your flesh
As rivers, never ending, come to rest.
"Well, then, I'll be going," he said
"No, no, not yet. Stay awhile.
The sun is barely
Touching the top of the pine.
Wait until the grass is dry;
Wait until the air is warm . . .
Wait .
The wood stair rail is smooth
His hand slides across it.
At the gate
She runs up to him
Falling against his overcoat.
She puts her hands in his pockets.
Then her spine pulls her back
Out of his arms.

He looks bewildered, then
The gate opens
Good by . . .
Good by.

Shall there, then, be a planting
Beyond the frost?
Who will drink from the crocus?

GREEN GYRE (2023)

Lament For You

A meditation of flowers turned
In their incomparable mute vanity
In the grey wind
And blackly tore their petals
Upward
Into trees

Some agony of time passing
May throw into this upward rain
The jeer such tenderness deserves
The flowers flaunt such orange music
As would turn pain to weeping
And gentle the blind world where a body
Is a knife thrown in terror

Their death might shake foundations
Shatter hope
In a last perfection

Do not meet these bright dreamers
That flicker in dark skies
Do not hold in the heart these cool flames
That drown all our listless sleeps in burning.

Circular Energy (2025)

A Just Thing

Wetter weather could only be
Under the sea, thought
This red-booted
Puddle scuffle, this
Janitor of the back-yard judgment day.
And so it was that sent
All the goldfish pouring
Into that rain spangled water.
And went back into the house with the empty evidence
6 years old, and no doubter of the miraculous.
And what disbelief.
Home from school that very same day
To find the sun's golden pennies everywhere
Dead bellied in the mud.

EYE FLOWER GREEN VIOLET (2007)

Husbandry

Into this valley of torment
I alone seem to be moving
Toward futures, with methodical intent.
It is a night-plagued and moon-chained plain
Where of the grass is bent
In long rippling to follow the icy planet,
If we turn our backs to look.
We do not turn. Straight ahead,
Our broken gazes on the earth
We till a furrow each, rich
For some other day's planting.
And behind, the grasses spring
In graceful rivers, where we have labored.

THE CRACK BETWEEN THE TWO WORLDS (1979)

Yggdrasil / The World Tree

Quiet I came into
The depths and dark places
I was frightened, and alone.
I put aside my mind and heard
The clamor of others — justice
Is a clawed hand — liberty A mockery
By the well-fed of the hungry.

The gates open — the knights
      ride out
And the beggar at the wall watches
Silent, for centuries,
Simple, a reminder
Of the holy brother.

War, war, death and ruin ...
Grandmother's well-tended garden
Shall be scattered and broken...

The walls close around them
Relieved of their iron clothing
They are but ourselves - they go
to their perfumed women

But the beggar goes to weep very
silently in the strewn garden

The Mountain Spring Flowers

In the high mountains
Hurt falls away, as though a
    stone
Dislodged by my foot
Rattled down crazily against
    the cliff
And I watched, until I could
    no longer see it.
Then turn around
The mountain spring flowers.

Prayer

In lordly assonance the thrice sung poet dragon
Lifts its head
And humbly asks
Its daily bread.

Old Confrontation

Our dreams are like the figures on the cards,
A Tarot deck of upside down desire.
We think by placing them in paste board hierarchy
and holding closely to their names and places
somehow to interweave them. But gilded, gaudy, and
disordered they come in caravan across our gutted mind.
They come to sing and to perform, a ritualistic and
insistent dance.
And they are all in costume and disguise, behind which
 our primeval selves peer, like proud and bestial kings
 with blackly radiant, impenetrable eye

GREEN PLANET

Irish Songs

The slight mounded green turf
Where the girls dance
dreaming.
Wet stones, salt rain,
The woman keening.

To My Husband Ned
For the New Year

Rainfall
Upward seed gesture
Axis of light
Turns the new year

A kiss
Suddenly opening the door of a warm room
The faint bitter aftertaste
Of a thousand perceptions

Old Songs

Senses slip into each other
A screen slides to reveal ecstatic form
Formula for color, emotion,
Fire warming, and death-flicker
Yellow, fire folding into the golden mean
Sun, brother to the night,
Holds up all that grows from a great height.

Turn in their silken clothes
Man, woman what have you to do
With one another, what of the other,
The transparencies of darkness, the creatures
At chasm-level,
The sea pulled along itself by a long pale desire?

Like a bird, they say, in answer;
It rises and goes up between us
Like the green hunter
In our silken clothing
We follow each other.
Sister and brother.

Going Out, The Wind Was Rising

La Belle Dame Sans Merci—the autumn weather
Drawing up, and high bright
As visions final flash before oblivion
Disguises the flesh-striped hand
The moldering, burning, disintegration of the
    failing year.

In the wind
There is the latticework
Black-it is trees, spiderwebs-clarity
The stream bed swelling
Small stones in rushing water
Underground, unknowing,
The seeds of summer are sprouting.

EYE FLOWER RED, BLUE

For Ned

I know the kind of love a blind man makes
Out of form, out of song
A mother full of trees
A cave open to the sea
A sailing, rush of weather, and a drying up,
A rock glyph the toe turns up.

Oh baby, come and dance with me
Among the operatic pigeons of the park
A cup, up to the top, it spills over
Into everything I mean.

Nefertiti's shape, the painted face
These thousand years baked into the ground.
Sometimes I wonder how it ends,
Our dance of flesh on bone...
The same? By lying down
Reaching in darkness for the shape

His great dark body outlines in stars.

> (Herein it is not represented,
> the ray of illuminated moment,
> frees the mind, gives self up
> to the rock song, gravel- patch
> the outworn body shape in
> patterns)

Who Will Break the Cherry Branch?

Who will break the cherry branch?
Who will draw a curtain
And let the light fall
Over body and across the floor When the night is past?

Oh love, let no parting be bitter
Lest we not meet again.
Let the past
Be like the Kaleidoscope of our days
Turning and changing.
But come to me in the winter weather
And we will walk out, and look at the stars.

They Flee From Me . . .

They flee from me, those unkempt dreams that were
Like women raving with their serpents hair.
To touch their fearful hands to see their pallor;
To turn round to their moon-rimmed stare
Would be to end the dreaming — but the dream
Sheds masked imaginings to gibber down
All places of pursuit. Their frightful scream
Palls, water-like, on footpaths, and I drown.
Through water-caves the carried bodies weave
These sightless women of my long-chilled wish.
Their hands are lovely, and they reach to save
Me from the endless darkness to the flesh.
And all caught in their glistening hair
Are child-times, and deeply passing is their stare.

The Convergence

Bach orders the room — its contents,
    its occupants,
And lends them sequence.
Webs of shadow
Formed in the long night
Dazzle and dissolve.

There is a dance
Which goes beyond us.
There is a line
Between the living and the dead
But so interwoven with harmony
Crossed like tracks on the beach.

The indeterminate germ puts
    forth new leaf
And itself unfolds, in the sun
Convoluted, opening, into the
    coming dark.
Bach ends his solitary dance
Beyond the window of our season
And we sit in the dark
    with quiet breathing.

TURNING TURNING (2025)

Mediterranean

In a glass bowl on a table
Are two oranges.
They are like the sun at the window:
Yellow-orange, round, plentiful.
And near the table the woman sits
considering a strand of hair...
Long hair, brown with orange, the sun
Entering into and caught in soft webbing.
It is she
Who has opened the curtains, she
Who places two oranges in a bowl.
She, in pale blue, will now rise
And walk down the beach
with a lovely motion.

The monastic imagery for the form of woman
Pale and chaste, but plentiful
Like the Italian maddone,
Brings us indolently to the sea
To the blue and absolute expanse of imagination.
In the word ocean, there is the far off cry of the gull.
To think of her, it is as though the scent
Of the orange
Remained with her as she walked in the foam.

We Were

There were, of course, echoes
For a long time afterwards-
Volcanoes spilled bright rubbish
And splinters of crystals turned up flashing.

We were the long shadow on the earth
We were sorrow, we walked,
We have been taken away,
The sun laughs through fountains of molten rock.
And the starlight is merry
Upon the multihued sand of the plain.

The steam of the sea rises in magnificent colors.

We were sorrow, but the cosmos is huge with joy.

Masquerade By Day

A golden face lies on a dimmed sheet—
Holes for eyes
Where some red-clothed thing
Gibbers in the broken lens;
Carmine lips flutter
Supplications to the cracked ceiling:
Strains from a jagged calliope
Punctured by the last frenzied blows of the fractured hour
That crumble the castle of desolate hilarity.

Oh mother of evil
(A pallid harlequin jerks near)
Ease us from presence,
Prepare us a void beyond the cell of atoms,
Rip from our skulls the white hot veins
That carry the red and screaming thought.
(A chequed creature gapes from its wooden mouth
A laugh that splinters on the floor,
Then merges into the window
And is gone, with its carnival coat caught on the sun.)

TAI CHI SYMBOL (2025)

Gather Together

Leaves lie, burning red into brown
Over them, the flowering tree
lifts its new season.
There is something here
A seed-pod.
Gather it

At the zoo,
Bright feathers, swept
Behind the aviary,
the tropical birds
found treasure
Which we wear.
And later

They fill our window
 Like flowers…

So much shining.

A snare for what I would keep
By looking softly
Open-hearted
Pebbled water rootwater
Filling up a well, just
so much,
no more.

It began as a stone
Thrown onto the pavement—
A smooth stone, white and warm,
With a shudder of heart-beat
In the dark plum color of the core.

Paper Chase With Motorcycle (2019)

It lay
Lengthening. As the night tattered and
caught up in the hair of the wind
Was carried away, desiring out the limbs and fingers
And she, beating and long
Rose into light carved like a pale rose
To fit the cupping hand
And what she knew of light
Was a petal-fall, imprinted on the arm
On the thigh.

And on an afternoon
She walked into her own whiteness
And slept white in the passing years.
Grew as the ringed ripple of a pool
And she held all, without touching.

To The Moan

To the moan which is heard on every side
Easy, the stark moon, with its clouds streaming
Women's hair, streaming
Man's desire, like a burning lodestone;
This call goes out even from the rocks Rivers of illumination,
    rose colored glasses for the multitudes
Oh, unrealistically piping, the small birds
In every bush, salvation armies of the soul
Spring
    out
        Hi

As I Came Home From the Store

As I came home from the store,
The people were walking against me
And the bell was calling come, come.
I taking my ease, enjoying the Xmas windows
In my own way
The Santa Claus plastic that goes on and off
(or on and on maybe?)
Tin trees with nests of wires in their hair
Here and there a child's drawing, but more often
An illuminated kewpie doll with wings
Of what mutated mythology some sociologist may say...
But I was saying-
They were Spanish people, they came on foot
As befits the worshipful, on bicycle
Boys with dark curls
Women with big stomachs leading three children
Like a candelabra, lifted up and close spaced.
Teenage tribal females their eyelids
Heavy with mascara, their identical purses
Swinging at the hips of identical taut skirts
Behind them the young men, hands in pockets,
Hair curled, taps on shoes...
And all by himself, an old fellow, making his way along
With a beautiful cane, shaking a little.
And the bell calls and calls
The carved oak door creaks open

Germination

Yellow, wind and worn laden.
Like a day of promise among familiar strangers
The mind turns in its thoughts.
The crackle, the sorrows, the virtue
Of dry leaf trail,
Of something old, fertile as loam
Something the dreamer paid to dream
At last coming round to pass
Nearly too ripe, almost putrid.
The trickled blood from the mouth,
Horrible, for blood to come from the mouth,
Slack and tender as a child in sleep.
It is a sleep near death coming upon me-
A dream of hands opening upon me
Dream of the soul's commerce with the flesh.

Dark Sabbath

The gardener is gone,
And now
I see the flow of will along the bough
And dew of crystal blossoms ring the night
Reverberating bright
Amid the shadows of the moonlight.

The ordered growing stains the very earth
With scent,
The black bough's bent
And from the stillness
Comes the singing of inhuman mirth.

PAPER CHASE #1 (2019)

At The Door

At the door to the dark room the pregnant woman stands.
Her dress pulls at her belly like a sunburst leading
out from her navel.
Her hair seems to plead with the air to let it lie glistening
over her shoulders.
She invites us into the room and brings us coffee
behaving like anyone else, but in the darkness her
petals will fade and her flowers shall burst inward.

Poetry As Speech

A tapestry broidered with flowers
Fruits of all seasons, and alighting birds
All the beasts of the plenteous earth . . .
So, If the gift of beautiful speech were given me,
Would I tapestry my god's temple
For pure love, and in the boldness of joy.
For the good god alone
Speech without this wrangling tongue
Pierced and cloyed in opposition;
Utter only the shape of the skin of silence.

Sri Ramakrishna

(he pointed to his body and he said, "a cage")
The house was tearing-
the grounds opened,
breaking into globular seed-pods,
fine lines,
hieroglyphs.

A dry rattle,
the tongue tied bones
thronged with parchment.
Waiting for some fertile squirming tear
that bursts the eye it came from.

In grief the light shines clearly,
say angels, who touch
their arching wings together.
They, having no eyes mourn
ceaselessly for those whose vision
caresses the outer edge of form,
the primary slate of color.

As woman opens unto lover,
this hole goes in and out as well.
This pigsty has become a church by now
The pigs go snorting through the pews
Caress the velvet silence with their dripping snouts
The parson cannot get them out...

You or no one can put down
Earth rising and falling
No help from any hand-
We all go along for the ride, and
Sister,
Roses or dandelions
It's all the same to me.
What they find has grown
Out of my pelvic bone
When dirt has pushed me down again
Like a big, fat, festering old seed.

And Then

Speak of sex, he said,
Unclouded by the intellect.
She thrust her tongue into his head —
A bed strewn with all the cast off
Garments of mischance,
Heat of the summer and the
Death of winter sleep.
My mind split into fragments.

Morning light making rainbows
Of lucid splinters,
Can you dance within the chaos?
And he answered Yes.
All songs became his as he passed.

THE TURNING WHEEL (2025)

Jazz Baby

Darling delicate glittering
Sweet ache as the mirror
Looses its reflected rainbows
And you come to me
Your brave little body
Barely clothed,
The chiffon hiding you — Oh your heavy jewelry
Your laugh hurts the same way —
They say they have something for it ...

There in the halls where Aphrodite
Hangs her clothes ...
Leaves her baubles carelessly around
Feathers —
Anything that shimmers
A soft rain from her long fingers
Where she walks there spring up
Persian carpets ...

She is so lonely in our era
These are the things she brings back to comfort her
Things that ache and ache
With a past unspent.

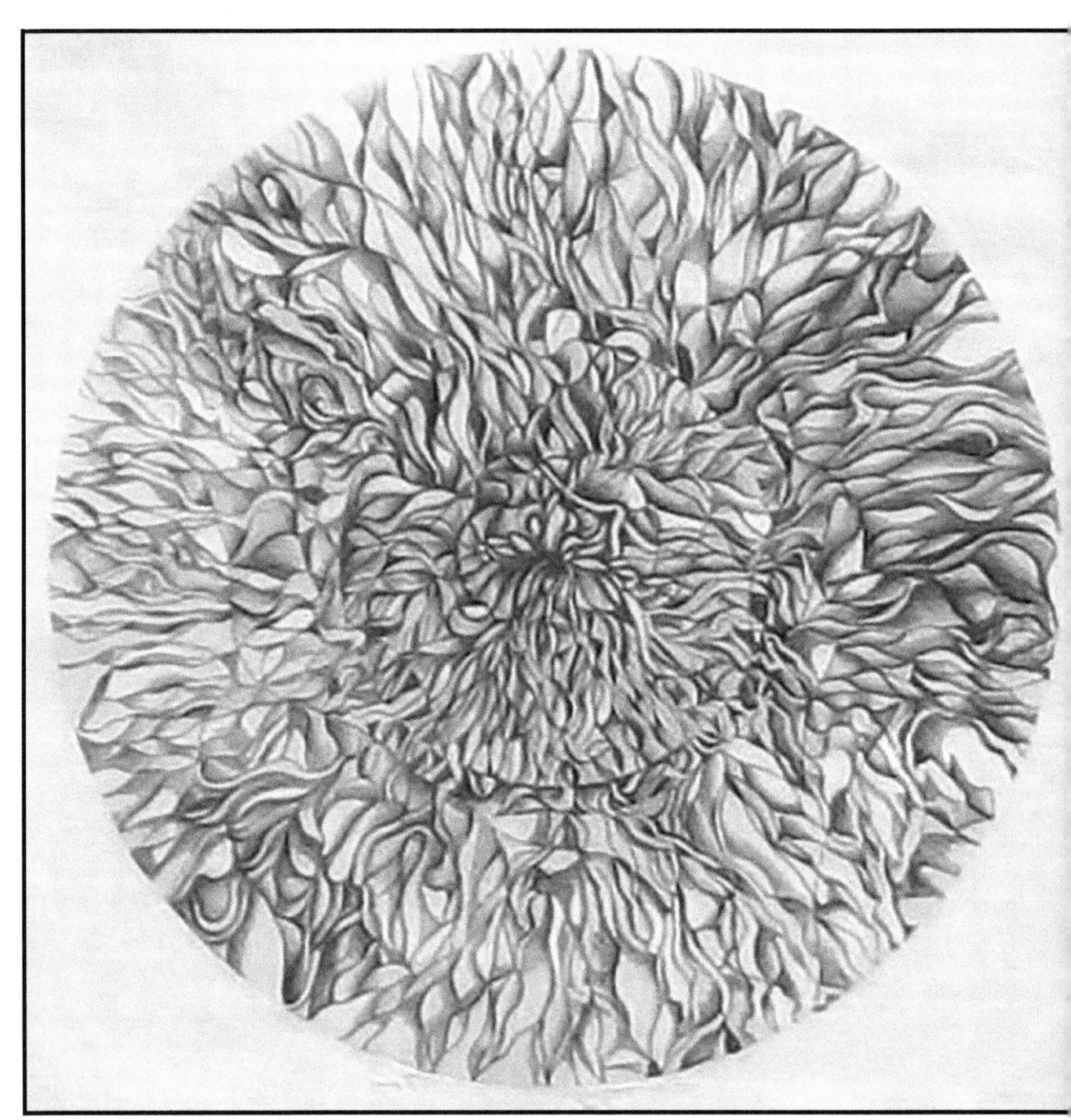

SEARCH (1978)

In Prehistoric Time

In Prehistoric time
Mother end father floated
In a green sea of submerged relationships.
It was a time of darkness, and of caves,
Of seaweed possibilities.
The fascination of the worm curled
Indelibly bright end tendrilled in the sluice of waters.

As things ask of the slime
For the materials of life
They will forget identities
Of monstrous bright shapes on which they feed.
So these sea-pictures fade
Become more dim, and more sophisticate.
And so come into the sun, shaking,
With their old newness,
Their wrinkled minds
Smoothed on the surface with the flood of light.

If only I did not dream.
It would be enough to comb the sun
With limbs that alter with the shapes of days
Sifting the light and dark
Of what I see ... a dance of flickering actualities.
But the worm, the Gorgon's seeking tongue.
The flame-haired mother crouched in caves of night
Or father standing with a bloody spear.

Mater Doloroso

Sorrowful lady, why wander
Beyond my call?
Here I have for you
Rare carved, cunning filigree
Intricacy
Without boundary

Beloved, (she answered)
Nowhere
Do I rest easy... It is
As though the flower withered
Before it has opened...
Do you not grieve for such loss?

But the shape, the fine ornamentation
The glass cup filled with love
The bell of times that surrounds us;
Can you depart from such a garden?

Oh such a wind do I see coming
As may sweep this very garden
And though I weep, I turn my face from soft words
And look to the cliff of the sea.

Vacant Lot

In the Queen Anne's Lace the birds
Rise and fall like dust, with desperate
Furious singing. They wheel
On a wind of social innuendoes
Among those gangling sisters.
Through their wings spray
Drops of the rainfall an hour past
In these high restless days of early spring.

Poem At The Cusp of the Year

Only like to the stone of circumstance
The weight born, now heavy now light
We take a measure made of steps
Placed in a pattern more within than chosen.

Performed
As the sea bird on its flights.
Each onto its kind
Man, his face
all imaginations outer skin
Changeling child
Goes where he will among the beasts.

The dance's
Exacting freedom
Still claims him.

THE SAILOR POET

Winter In San Francisco

When the windwoman sways her nervous body
Into the bay,
In that Little space,
There is a hesitancy, a leafy thought
of following after.
Then the becalmed slackening
Into a customary position
As it seems she has passed on.
Resting again against the air
The day stands again in its indolent fragility.
But it is only the inertia of our old habit
That has etched this summer in permanence.
With the careless hem of her energy
She draws the light into the sea
And dwindles it.
Then, at the very sailmost horizon
Of tiny balancing
She pivots
And comes keening and splintering
Through the voices
Of our astonished yearning.

Each Coat a Color, Each Room a View

Many rooms has my father's mansion, muy casas
Each room made because it was needed
Each window made because the wall was transparent

From places we have never been which our forefathers destroyed
 and our foremothers did not protect because they didn't go to the
same church
Every thing was brought to here because
Before here was nothing but the sand and the water below the sand
and the rocks with their thousand colors and the plants and the
insects and the birds and the lizard? and the sky and the water
in it and the stars.

The stars came here.
I'm damn sure John (Wayne) came here.
Orion came here.
The stars still come here.

This is the place made out of people made this.
I'm homesick.

A Dervish in the Park

Turns turns staggers
Falls with a clatter and a crack.
I skitter over to it,
A leaf on the wind
Dancing sideways.
Its eyes are slits
In a metallic mask
The mask is gold
It is made of
Many rituals.
Here and there I can see the joins—
The Mayan with Mines
The African boar with the Indian Mother
Kali calling to Quetzalcoatl—
There is dust lying over its eyes.
It shudders—
The body in its thin skirt of flesh
The ancient bones
Whisper to each other.
In old anarchy.
Lies there, rocking and moaning
Its tongue like a snake
Darting out with separate life
It is like no old bird, stranded
With its foul-weather wings
Useless and broken
In the California sun.
Until a man in grey coveralls
Comes and sweeps it into a bag
Along with the leaves.
All that's left is a speck
Of glittering golden blood.

SPIRAL PLANET (2010)

Into The Secret

Into the secret magnificence of love we go
             following, following
Forms upon walls, caves of flickering,
Seeking the root, the fleshy wood, the form of the
             Other.

The innocence of pleasure
A long line dance
Over the hill we passed,
And it was
Follow the leader round the rain bell
The cloud manna, the soul pasture,
Down, round, into the earth —
In the fury of the dance ... Do not
Be deceived, the heart
Is gnome like.

These caves of fire-studded night
Are our inheritance.
Palatial underground of old mythology
Dazzles us.
We come as strangers to ourselves.

Crow Woman

Crow-woman curves her hands around a staff
And dances,
Her feet press the sodden ground.
Her face twists, her shoulders hunch.
Her body is old.
The moss grows between her feet
Before she can step again.
She cuts the earth with the blows of her walking stick,
From the blows grow red blood flowers ...
The sky quivers,
The tide turns,
Drawing along its glowing fishes.
Crow-woman grows darker and more bent
Until only her breath remains
Seen as the crucible
Of a flaming stone.
I see crow-woman take her bones apart
And toss them on the fire like sticks of wood.
I see her rise up in her golden plumes
And bear toward the sun.

Edward (a.k.a. Ned) Millett has been an artist since he was sixteen. A native San Franciscan, he knew Bob Kaufman, meditated with Allan Ginsberg at Dharmadhatu in 1970, and has been a friend of Jack Hirschman (S.F.'s Poet Laureate 2006-07) since 1976. Ned was one of the first Bay Area artists to use the mandala extensively in his work (1962). He had a show with Susan Cervantes, S.F.'s preeminent muralist, at the Live Worms Gallery in January, 2008, and filled an entire room for a show at the Chinese Art Museum in Oakland, CA. He has a B.F.A. in fine art painting from the San Francisco Art Institute and was also in their masters program. (1965-1970). *[Photo by Philip Galgioni, 19 April 1970.]*

www.ingramcontent.com/pod-product-compliance
Lightning Source LLC
Chambersburg PA
CBHW040009080526
44586CB00028B/2940